BRITAIN'S 🏰 HERITAGE

Express Trains

Tim Bryan

AMBERLEY

Acknowledgements

The author and publisher would like to thank the following people/organisations for permission to use copyright material in this book: STEAM: Museum of the Great Western Railway, Swindon, Science & Society Picture Library, Mike Freeman, Great Central Railwayana Auctions, Ashley Smith, Roger Cruse of the Bluebell Railway Museum Archive, Paul Childs/Railway Heritage Trust, Venice Simplon-Orient-Express Ltd, Virgin Trains East Coast, Great Western Trust, David Christie, 53A Models of Hull Collection, Pete Wilcox and the British Motor Industry Heritage Trust. Thanks to Adrian Harrison for the cover image. All other images are from the author's collection.

Every attempt has been made to seek permission for copyright material used in this book. However, if we have inadvertently used copyright material without permission/ acknowledgement we apologise and we will make the necessary correction at the first opportunity.

First published 2017

Amberley Publishing
The Hill, Stroud
Gloucestershire, GL5 4EP

www.amberley-books.com

Copyright © Tim Bryan, 2017

The right of Tim Bryan to be identified as the Author of this work has been asserted in accordance with the Copyrights, Designs and Patents Act 1988.

ISBN 978 1 4456 6878 9 (paperback)
ISBN 978 1 4456 6879 6 (ebook)

British Library Cataloguing in Publication Data.
A catalogue record for this book is available from the British Library.

Printed in the UK.

Contents

1
Introduction

The most glamorous services run by railway companies were the high speed expresses. Often named, these premier trains were the fastest and most luxurious services offered by railways and generated much publicity, especially in the 1920s and 1930s, when such trains also regularly broke speed records.

By far the most famous express services were the trains whose names still resonate with the public today such as the 'Flying Scotsman', the 'Royal Scot', the 'Cornish Riviera Limited' and the 'Atlantic Coast Express'. These and luxurious 'Pullman' services featured the newest and fastest locomotives and the most up-to-date and comfortable rolling stock. Although most named trains were suspended in wartime, more than eighty were still in operation by 1956 on British Railways.

In addition to the named trains, the 'Big Four' railways, which were created in 1923, and later the nationalised British Railways operated many other un-named express services across the network, linking London and major towns and cities, as well as well-known holiday destinations around the coast. There were also specialised express services that were an important part of the railway timetable; these included boat trains linking ocean terminals and the capital, overnight sleepers, fast mail trains and excursion specials.

A sepia postcard view of LNER A4 Pacific No. 4492 *Dominion of New Zealand* at the head of the company's premier train, the 'Flying Scotsman'.

The 'Flying Dutchman' was one of the earliest named trains to run on British railways. Named after a racehorse that had won the Derby and St Leger in 1849, the Paddington–Exeter express ran over broad-gauge lines operated by the Great Western and Bristol & Exeter Railways until May 1892.

No. 21C123 *Blackmore Vale* hauls a 'Golden Arrow' dining car train at Ketches Wood on the Bluebell Railway on 18 October 2003. (Roger Cruse, Bluebell Railway Museum Archive)

Always at the vanguard of technological development, railways introduced many innovations that improved express train speeds and journey times. In addition, of course, to the best locomotives these services had rolling stock and passenger facilities of the highest quality, making a journey on an express in the golden age of steam an experience not to be missed for the well-heeled traveller.

The decline of steam and the introduction of the British Railways Modernisation plan in 1954, while leading to a dramatic reduction of Britain's railway network, was also intended to usher in an age of fast modern 'Intercity' express travel. Many of the most famous expresses of the steam age vanished in the 1970s and today only a few have survived; faster diesel and electric trains now mean that most train services are considerably faster than their predecessors, even though the overall level of comfort provided for passengers does not match that of the best expresses of the past.

The opening of the Channel Tunnel in 1994 saw the beginning of a new era of high-speed express trains running between London and the Continent. Eurostar trains on this side of the Channel still, however, run on lines largely built in the Victorian era and, until other new routes like HS2 are finally built, a true renaissance of high-speed express services in Britain may well still be some time in the future.

Left: No. 6100 *Royal Scot* in full flight on the express of the same name. After 1933, larger and more powerful Princess Royal and Coronation engines replaced Royal Scot engines on the premier LMS express.
Below: Eurostar express trains wait under the William Barlow-designed train shed at St Pancras station, awaiting departure for the Continent. (Paul Childs & Railway Heritage Trust)

2
Four Famous Expresses

Running on the East Coast Main Line from London to Edinburgh, the 'Flying Scotsman' is probably the most famous express in the world. The service was only given this name officially in 1924, despite making its daily 10.00 a.m. departure from London King's Cross since 1862; a southbound service departed from Edinburgh Waverley at the same time. It was originally known as the 'Special Scotch Express' and made the 392-mile journey in 10 ½ hours, pausing at York for half an hour to allow passengers to eat a leisurely lunch in the station dining room. After 1900, dining cars were introduced and the stop was cut to just ten minutes.

Until 1923, when the London & North Eastern Railway was created as one of the 'Big Four' railways, the service had been run jointly by the Great Northern, North Eastern

Above: This early postcard shows the predecessor of the 'Flying Scotsman', the 'Flying Scotchman', being hauled by Great Northern Railway 4-4-2 No. 990 *Henry Oakley*. Built in 1898, the engine is now in the collection of the National Railway Museum. (STEAM)
Right: Gresley A1 Pacific No. 2563 *William Whitelaw*, built at Doncaster in 1924, departs from London King's Cross with the 'Flying Scotsman' service.

and North British Railways, who competed with the London & North Western and Caledonian railways for Anglo-Scottish traffic. Following races between both groupings on the East and West Coast main lines in 1888 and 1895, it was agreed that journey times for both routes should be fixed at 8 ½ hours on both lines, a timing that amazingly continued until 1932.

In 1923, Sir Nigel Gresley, Chief Mechanical Engineer of the LNER, introduced his new powerful A1 Pacific class locomotives; most were named after famous racehorses, but confusingly the third in the class was called *Flying Scotsman*. To make matters worse, it was not until the following year that the LNER made the name of the express official, with the 'train named after the engine that was named after the train' as author Andrew Martin concluded.

To inaugurate the 'new' service, the company introduced improved carriages but it was not until 1928 that more dramatic improvements were made. In May the service became non-stop from London to Edinburgh during the summer months, although the 8 ½ hour timing remained. At the time, the run was the longest non-stop rail journey in the world and a journey time of over 8 hours was too much for one crew alone. To overcome this, a locomotive tender with a corridor was introduced, enabling a second fresh crew to take over north of York without the train having to stop. The new train also had luxurious new carriages that included a 'Ladies' Retiring Room', hairdressing salon and cocktail bar, described at the time as 'ultra-modern' and 'the pleasantest of haunts to spend half an hour'.

The service was finally accelerated and the journey time reduced to 7 ½ hours in 1932, with a further ten minutes being cut in 1938. The express was one of a few that continued to run throughout the Second World War, although it seldom carried a headboard during the conflict. In 1948, the non-stop service was discontinued but the train continued to be steam hauled until 1958, when diesel traction finally took over. Four years later the Eastern Region's premier express was handed over to new Deltic diesels that were capable of maintaining a journey time of 5 hours 20 minutes.

HST 125 diesels took over the 'Flying Scotsman' service in 1982 but the 10 a.m. departure from King's Cross was abandoned and, although the famous name has continued to be used by companies on the East Coast Main Line franchise, the train now only runs from North to South, leaving Edinburgh at 5.40 in the morning and taking just four hours to reach London. There is no special service in the opposite direction.

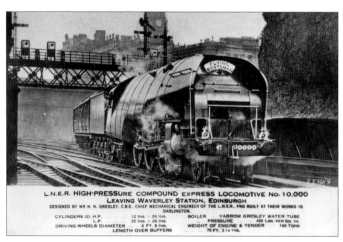

L.N.E.R. HIGH-PRESSURE COMPOUND EXPRESS LOCOMOTIVE No. 10.000
LEAVING WAVERLEY STATION, EDINBURGH
DESIGNED BY MR H. N. GRESLEY, C.B.E. CHIEF MECHANICAL ENGINEER OF THE L.N.E.R. AND BUILT AT THEIR WORKS IN DARLINGTON.

CYLINDERS (2), H.P.	12 INS. × 26 INS.	BOILER	YARROW GRESLEY WATER TUBE
L.P.	20 INS. × 26 INS.	PRESSURE	450 LBS. PER SQ. IN.
DRIVING WHEELS DIAMETER	6 FT. 8 INS.	WEIGHT OF ENGINE & TENDER	166 TONS
	LENGTH OVER BUFFERS	75 FT. 3 ½ INS.	

Instead of the normal Gresley Pacific, the southbound 'Flying Scotsman', leaving Edinburgh Waverley, is hauled by the massive bulk of the experimental 4-6-4 Hush-Hush engine. Built in 1929 it featured a high-pressure marine-type boiler, operating at 450 psi. The engine was eventually rebuilt with a conventional boiler in 1937.

Did you know?

What's in a name? It is thought that the adoption of names for train services was a continuation of a practice applied to the original horse-drawn stagecoaches the railways rapidly replaced in the 1830s and 1840s. Train names reflected fashion and events, too; the 'Belle' name adopted by the Southern on a number of its expresses was typical of the Art Deco 1930s.

Across the Pennines, the premier express train running on the West Coast Main line from London to Scotland was the 'Royal Scot'. This famous express did not carry this name officially until July 1927, although the train had a long tradition that dated back to 10.00 a.m. on 1 June 1862, when the first train using that route left Euston for Glasgow and Edinburgh. Before Grouping, the express was run by the London & North Western Railway as far as Carlisle,

The most famous headboard of all? This style of headboard was used on the *Flying Scotsman* from June 1950 onwards and sold at auction in 2015 for £8,600. (Great Central Railwayana Auctions)

where the Caledonian Railway took over for the final leg of the journey. Like their rivals on the East Coast, the two companies were also subject to the agreed minimum journey time of 8 ½ hours, removing the competition that had characterised the 'Race to the North'.

By 1910, the 10.00 a.m. departure from Euston had the clumsy title of the 'Glasgow, Edinburgh, Dundee and Aberdeen Luncheon and Dining Car Express' and only ran as a joint train as far as Crewe, having already called at Willesden and Rugby. The train was then divided with carriages from Bristol added to the Glasgow portion of the express, which then left five minutes ahead of the Edinburgh train and also acquired through coaches for Aberdeen. This arrangement was reinstated after the First World War and continued until March 1925, when the new London Midland & Scottish company separated the two services, with the Glasgow train having a scheduled departure of 10.00 a.m. and its sister train to Edinburgh leaving eight minutes later.

This important change was followed in July 1927 by a more dramatic development: the adoption of the official 'Royal Scot' title for the 10.00 a.m. service. More significant was the fact

The naming of the Virgin Trains 'Flying Scotsman' service in October 2015, with Scottish First Minister Nicola Sturgeon and Virgin Trains East Coast Managing Director David Horne. (Virgin Trains East Coast/Creative Commons licence)

Royal Scot class No. 6103 *Royal Scots Fusilier* has just taken water at Bushey troughs on its way to Scotland with the 'Royal Scot' service.

The massive boiler of Fowler No. 6100 *Royal Scot* is prominent in this 1920s postcard view of the engine, hauling the express of the same name.

that the train now ran non-stop to Carnforth – a journey of 236 miles. The introduction of new 4-6-0 Fowler-designed Royal Scot class locomotives in September meant that the LMS was now able to run the train non-stop to Carlisle, a distance of almost 300 miles. The company was then able to claim the longest non-stop run record, a title snatched from them the following year with the introduction of the 'Flying Scotsman's corridor tender. The introduction of the larger Princess Royal and, later, Princess Coronation (or 'Duchess') class locomotives enabled the LMS to compete with the LNER in the 1930s with a 7-hour journey time to Glasgow.

The Royal Scot was not given its official name back until three years after the end of the Second World War; the 7-hour pre-war journey time was never matched, and its traditional 10.00 departure time was changed on a number of occasions to 9.05 a.m., 9.50 a.m. and 10.05 a.m. Steam traction was still largely the norm during the 1950s, although diesel locomotives were used increasingly during the period. The gradual electrification of the West Coast Main Line meant that electric locomotives hauled the train to Crewe after 1966, although the full conversion of the route to Glasgow was not completed until 1974. The 'Royal Scot' name was dropped in 2003 and the journey from Euston to Glasgow now takes around 4 ½ hours.

One of the few express trains to retain its original name is the 'Cornish Riviera Express', run between London and Penzance. The train, now operated by a company that has itself

This very plain style of headboard was carried on the 'Royal Scot' express in the early 1950's. (Great Central Railwayana Auctions)

revived the old Great Western Railway name, began life in July 1904 but only acquired its name a month later, following a competition in the *Railway Magazine*. More than a thousand people made suggestions, including the 'Riviera Express' and the 'Cornish Riviera Limited'. The former was pronounced the winner, but the GWR added the prefix 'Cornish', no doubt to add weight to their efforts to promote the Royal Duchy as a tourist destination. To many staff, the train was always known as the 'Limited' (referring to limited stops en route) or the '10.30 Limited', reflecting its departure time from Paddington.

When the train was introduced, it originally left the capital at 10.10 a.m. and ran non-stop to Plymouth via Bristol, taking 4 hours 25 minutes for this journey – the longest non-stop run on British railways at the time. The service then stopped at principal Cornish stations before arriving at Penzance at 5.10 p.m. Running only in the summer until 1906, the train initially included five carriages and a dining car but, by the 1930s, it could have as many as sixteen

Left: The 'Cornish Riviera Express' is pictured running along the coast between Exeter and Dawlish. Variations of this particular image were used in various forms for Great Western publicity in the 1930s.

Below: This illustration, reproduced from a children's book of the 1920s, was based on a photograph of GWR King class locomotive, No. 6000 *King George V*, at the head of the 'Cornish Riviera Express'.

coaches weighing over 575 tons. The opening of a new route via Castle Cary in 1906 cut 20 miles from the route and enabled the journey time to be cut to just over 4 hours.

From that date the 'Cornish Riviera Express' ran all year, leaving Paddington at 10.30 a.m., interrupted only by the Great War and coal shortages in the winter of 1946/47. A return train departed from Penzance at 10.00 a.m. To maintain its tight timing and to serve intermediate stations, the train was divided into portions and slip coaches were detached at Westbury, Taunton, Exeter, Par, Truro and St Erth, serving holiday destinations such as Weymouth, Ilfracombe, Newquay, Falmouth and St Ives. Undoubtedly the years between the two World Wars were a high point for the train; in 1923, C. B. Collett's new powerful Castle class locomotives were introduced and, in 1929, to mark the Silver Jubilee of the train, the GWR invested in new luxurious rolling stock. Six years later, to mark the 100th anniversary of the railway, even larger 'Centenary' carriage stock was introduced, with comfort and facilities rivalling anything offered on the Pullman services run by other Big Four companies.

The 'Limited' continued to run throughout the Second World War, and remained steam hauled until the late 1950s, when Swindon-built diesel-hydraulic engines were introduced on the service. The express ceased to be locomotive-hauled in 1981, when high speed trains were introduced; they remain in use today, although the service no longer runs non-stop,

The 'Cornish Riviera Express' headboard carried by a British Railways Warship class diesel-hydraulic locomotive in this 1950s postcard features the coat of arms of the Royal Duchy. (STEAM)

Some enthusiasts have argued that the front end of the Southern Railway Lord Nelson class looked rather ugly without the smoke deflectors that were added in the late 1920s. The engines had a reputation for poor steaming, despite being dubbed the most powerful locomotive in the world when first constructed. (STEAM)

Famous " Atlantic Coast Express" leaving Waterloo for Devon and North Cornwall, drawn by the " LORD NELSON " (Southern Railway). Britain's most powerful passenger Engine.

instead calling at Reading, Exeter, Plymouth and numerous Cornish stations. The journey time has improved dramatically from the days of steam, however, with Penzance now being reached in just over 5 hours.

During busy summer months, the demand for seats on the 'Cornish Riviera Express' meant that additional relief trains often needed to be run. The same could be said for its Southern Railway rival, the 'Atlantic Coast Express', which on summer weekdays could consist of two separate trains and on Saturdays might even increase to five or six. The Southern had run an express to the West Country that left Waterloo at 11.00 a.m. since the Grouping, continuing a service that had been operated by the London & South Western since 1900. The 'North Cornwall and Bude Express' lost its title in 1914 and it was not until three years after the creation of the Big Four that the new name was adopted.

While the Great Western used slip coaches to serve intermediate stations on its Cornish Riviera route, the Southern relied on smart working by staff to allow the detaching of carriages for destinations at various locations. The passenger joining the train at Waterloo needed to ensure that they were in the correct coach, since the train would be formed into various 'portions'. By the late 1920s, it had nine; these served Ilfracombe, Torrington, Plymouth, Padstow, Bude, Sidmouth, Exmouth and Exeter itself. Two restaurant cars, detached at Exeter, completed the train. The various component parts of the service reached their destinations in Devon and Cornwall at regular intervals, being marshalled into other trains; however, the final and most 'Atlantic' portion of the train serving Plymouth, Bude and Padstow did not reach the end of the line at the Cornish terminus of Padstow until 5.37 p.m.

A gloomy post-war postcard view of Merchant Navy class Pacific *Elders Fyffe* on the Down 'Atlantic Coast Express'. The engine was not built until March 1945 but still carries the words 'Southern' on its tender.

Did you know?

Like the 'Cornish Riviera Express', the name of the 'Atlantic Coast Express' was also chosen by a competition. Unlike the GWR, who had advertised in the *Railway Magazine*, the Southern instead ran a competition for staff, and the winner was a guard from Woking, Mr F. Rowland, who won three guineas for his suggestion of 'Atlantic Coast Express'. Tragically Rowland was killed in a shunting accident six years later.

Like many expresses operated by the Big Four, the 'Atlantic Coast Express' lost its name during the Second World War, but was reintroduced immediately afterwards. The introduction of Bulleid Merchant Navy and lighter West Country Pacific locomotives led to improvements in journey times and train speeds. With nationalisation, the 'ACE' became one of the most important expresses on the Southern region. The 1950s saw further improvements to the timetable, but gains were short-lived. After 1960 road competition badly affected holiday business, and the transfer of lines west of Exeter to the Western Region in 1963 led to the withdrawal of some portions of the train. The end came the following year, when the final 'Atlantic Coast Express' service was run on 5 September 1964. The subsequent closure of much of the route in the West Country following the Beeching report meant that a revived version of the train reintroduced by First Great Western in 2008 runs on the old GWR route to Newquay, a destination not served by the original train.

Southern Railway West Country class 4-6-2 *Blackmoor Vale* is captured by an unknown photographer when complete with 'Atlantic Coast Express' headboard at the Bluebell Railway. The 1946-built engine was withdrawn from traffic in 2010 and is currently under restoration.

3
Pullman Luxury

For many, the epitome of luxury express train travel were the stylish Pullman carriages that ran on many of the most famous express trains on British railways from the 1870s onwards. While Great Britain can rightly claim to be the birthplace of the railway, the Pullman Car Company was actually an American concern, founded by George Mortimer Pullman, who developed the idea of building luxury carriages in the United States before exporting the idea to Britain in 1873. That year Pullman signed an agreement with the Midland Railway to build and run Pullman 'cars' (the American term for carriages) on a fifteen-year contract. In return, passengers using Pullman trains would be charged a supplement to their normal fare. This arrangement was soon adopted by many other British railways, with only a few like the GWR not using Pullman stock on their trains.

The distinctive design of Pullman rolling stock owed much to the American origins of the company; the carriage bodies were straight-sided rather than curved, and doors opened inwards rather than outwards. Early in the twentieth century, the familiar livery of umber brown and cream with a white roof was standardised; first class cars were named, usually after royalty, precious stones or girls' names.

The distinctive exteriors of Pullman stock were matched by their plush and exotic interiors. Only the best materials were used, and those built in the 1920s and 1930s featured Art Deco style panelling in woods such as mahogany, sandalwood and walnut, decorated with marquetry designs. Most first class accommodation was in the form of open 'Parlour cars' that featured freestanding upholstered chairs rather than conventional carriage seats, separated by tables decorated with a trademark lamp and a crisp white tablecloth. Naturally, trains also included kitchen cars to supply the sumptuous meals served to passengers and, in some cases, a bar car where travellers could sip cocktails on the move.

Although this picture of the interior of a Belmond British Pullman car was taken in 2010, this scene could be from the golden age of rail travel in the 1930s. (Venice-Simplon-Orient Express Ltd)

The 'Golden Arrow' train normally consisted of ten Pullman cars, with additional vans for passenger luggage. This 1920s view shows Lord Nelson class engine No. 854 *Howard of Effingham.*

Many of the most famous Pullman services were boat trains – expresses timed to connect with steamship services to the Continent. Of these, 'The Golden Arrow', operated by the Southern, is perhaps the best known. Uniquely, the train provided a direct route between London and the Gare du Nord in Paris, with Pullman stock used on either side of the English Channel. It was linked by a special steamer, the SS *Canterbury*, which carried passengers from Dover to Calais. From the Gare Maritime station there, the train, named the 'Fleche d'Or' in France, ran the 156 miles to Paris. The Nord Company had introduced the French service in 1926, but it was three years before the Southern Railway provided a matching service on the English side of the Channel. The express began as an all first class Pullman service, but the effects of the Great Depression following the Wall Street Crash in 1929 led to a decrease in cross-Channel traffic. As a result ordinary first and third class carriages were added to the train.

The SS *Canterbury* was built by Berry of Dumbarton in 1929 specially for the Southern Railway's 'Golden Arrow' service. At the outbreak of the Second World the *Canterbury* was converted into a troopship and went on to help evacuate troops at Dunkirk. It was finally scrapped in 1965.

The busy and confused scene at Dover Marine station on 1 April 1946 on the occasion of the first post-war trial of the 'Golden Arrow' service. (STEAM)

Leaving Victoria at 11 a.m., the traveller could be in the French capital by late afternoon and there is no doubt that the 'Golden Arrow' was *the* glamour train on British railways; it carried film stars, politicians, celebrities and the wealthy to Paris, from where they could join other long-distance trains like the Orient Express. The train did not run during the dark days of the Second World War, but was reinstated in 1946 and continued to be steam-hauled until 1961, when the service was electrified. The last 'Golden Arrow' finally ran on 30 September 1972.

By 1926 the Southern had more than sixty Pullman cars on in use on services run from London to Sussex coastal destinations, including Brighton, Newhaven and Hastings. The 'Southern Belle' was a train that continued a tradition of Pullman trains run on the Brighton line, dating back to December 1881 when the 'Pullman Limited Express' was inaugurated by the London, Brighton & South Coast Railway. In 1908 it was replaced by the 'Southern Belle', which was

A recreation of the 'Golden Arrow' using original Pullman stock on the Bluebell Railway on a dining train. The locomotive is an SR U class 2-6-0, built in 1931. (Ashley Smith)

claimed at the time to be the 'world's most luxurious train'. The service continued to be successful after Grouping, but the decision to electrify the Brighton line in 1929 cast doubt on the future of the steam-hauled express. Both the Southern and the Pullman Car Company were anxious to maintain the train, and so agreement was reached to build three new all-electric Pullman trains, each consisting of just five carriages.

Constructed in 1932, the stock retained the luxurious standards seen in conventional Pullman carriages with a 'motor' car at either end, along with the usual high quality catering. Leaving Victoria at 11 a.m., there were additional departures from the capital at 3.00 p.m. and 7.00 p.m., with return services leaving the Sussex resort at 1.25 p.m., 5.25 p.m. and 9.25 p.m. The electric trains were able to complete the journey in just an hour, and the 'Southern Belle' and other high-speed services helped boost the fortunes of Brighton as a resort

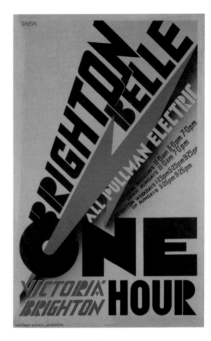

Above right: A poster produced to promote the 'Brighton Belle' train in 1934. The lightning bolt and lettering in the artwork by Charles Shepherd were intended to demonstrate the speed and modernity of the service. (SSPL)

Below: Dappled sunlight streaming through the roof at Victoria highlights the leading carriage of the 'Brighton Belle' in this undated postcard view of the train.

The 'Brighton Belle' races through Clapham Junction on 2 September 1968. (Pete Wilcox)

The 'Bournemouth Belle' Pullman service ran daily to the south coast resort from Waterloo. In this postcard view, the train is hauled by Lord Nelson class 4-6-0 No. 862 *Lord Collingwood*. (STEAM)

Did you know?

The GWR was conspicuous in not using Pullman cars on its services. The company briefly used them on boat trains between London and Plymouth in May 1929 and some months later inaugurated the non-stop 'Torquay Pullman' service between Paddington, Paignton and Torquay. Lasting less than a year, no further Pullman expresses ran on GWR lines until after nationalisation, when the 'South Wales Pullman' was introduced in 1955. Instead of using Pullman stock, the GWR built its own 'super saloons', a number of which still survive on heritage railways.

and commuter destination. It was not a surprise then when, in June 1934, the express was renamed the 'Brighton Belle', a name it would carry until the end.

The service was suspended during the Second World War when one of the units was badly damaged in an air raid; reinstated in 1946, the 'Brighton Belle' continued to operate much as it had done before the war, retaining its familiar umber-and-cream livery. In 1963 an additional round trip was added but the rolling stock began to look increasingly old-fashioned and, five years later, British Railways refurbished the trains, replacing the traditional Pullman livery with BR blue-and-grey colours. This facelift provided a brief reprieve for the 'Belle', but falling passenger numbers and increasing maintenance costs led to its withdrawal in 1972.

The other Big Four railway to make extensive use of Pullman stock was the London & North Eastern Railway. This was in no small part due to the fact that, in 1923, the newly created company found itself saddled with a long-term contract with Pullman that had

When introduced by the LNER in the 1920's the *'Hook Continental'* included at least two Pullman carriages in the train. This headboard dates from 1951 and the back is marked 'Return to Stratford'. (Great Central Railwayana Auctions)

been agreed by the Great Eastern Railway, one of the companies absorbed into the new group. While Pullman cars had been used on boat trains running between London and Parkeston Quay, they were less profitable on other services. New management was therefore keen to quickly find a more profitable use for the Pullman stock, with years still to run on the contract.

Removing all the carriages from GER lines except those used on boat trains, the LNER began introducing new all-Pullman trains on its services to Yorkshire and further North. The first service to be introduced in 1923 was the 'Harrogate Pullman', which left King's Cross at 11.15 a.m. The train did not terminate at the Yorkshire Spa town, but instead continued on to Newcastle, from where the southbound service also started. Two years later, the train ran as far as Edinburgh,

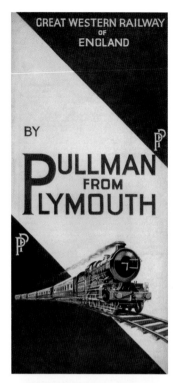

a journey of 8 hours 35 minutes. The same year, the 'West Riding Pullman' was introduced, serving Leeds and Bradford, and was followed in 1928 by the 'Queen of Scots', a service featuring brand-new Pullman cars. This express ran to Glasgow and Edinburgh via Leeds, a route that required footplate crews to work hard to achieve tight timings and arrive punctually, especially after 1932 when the agreement between the LMS and LNER over Anglo-Scottish services was abandoned. Suspended during the Second World War, the 'Queen of Scots' was reinstated in BR days and continued until 1964, when it was renamed the 'White Rose'.

The circuitous route and modest journey times of these Pullman trains serving the North East, especially after the introduction of streamlined expresses like the 'Silver Jubilee' and the 'Coronation', led to pressure

Left: The front cover of a handbill advertising the very short-lived Pullman service operated by the GWR and serving ocean liner passengers at Plymouth. The reference to 'Great Western Railway of England' indicates that it was distributed to travellers in the USA. (Great Western Trust Didcot)

Below: The title of this painting reproduced in a 1920s children's book is *Yorkshire Pullman*, although it could well have been a number of LNER Pullman services run in the 1920s.

from the business community and Pullman company to improve matters. New Pullman rolling stock was ordered for the East Coast Main Line in 1939 but was not completed until 1951, by which time the decision had been made to use it on the 'Golden Arrow' instead. Travellers on what had become the Eastern Region of British Railways instead saw in 1948 the introduction of a new train using existing carriages called the 'Tees-Tyne Pullman' that, by the early 1950s, had cut journey times from Newcastle to the capital to under 5 hours. By the time the train was removed from timetables in 1976, the trip had been reduced further to fewer than 4 hours.

The Pullman Company retained control over its franchise until 1954, when British Railways gained control of the operation, a process that was completed in 1962 when it was absorbed into the British Railways Board. BR continued to operate Pullman services

Did you know?

In 1960 Pullman travel made a brief resurgence in the form of the diesel-powered 'Blue Pullman' trains. Three separate services were eventually run, with the aim of serving a business clientele who wished to travel to London from the provinces. Running on the Western Region of British Railways with their distinctive blue livery, the trains linked Bristol, South Wales and Birmingham. All three trains were withdrawn by 1973.

A Western Region Pullman train stands ready to depart at Paddington station on 5 September 1962. (David Christie)

but, with the exception of the 'Blue Pullman' trains introduced in the early 1960's, they were often a shadow of the old trains. By then the airliner had taken over as the preferred option for those seeking the quickest and most glamorous way to travel. In British Railways days, there were still a number of trains that retained the 'Pullman' brand, although the rolling stock used was normally standard BR carriages fitted out to a higher specification rather than the distinctive umber-and-cream cars used in earlier times. Today, while some Pullman cars have been preserved by heritage railways, many have been purchased and refurbished by companies such as VSOE (Venice Simplon Orient Express) and used on luxury excursions and steam-hauled express trains.

A dramatic head-on view of No. 60163 *Tornado* speeding through with a 'Belmond British Pullman' train on 6 February 2016. (Ashley Smith)

4
Speed and Streamliners

In the years after the First World War rivalry between railways and a drive for progress and development led to a new breed of express trains that reflected an era of experimentation, culminating in the introduction of a number of high-speed streamlined services.

These new trains looked very different to those that had gone before; in the 1920s, all the new Big Four railways had spent time recovering from the war and at least some of the express locomotives built in that era still had their roots in pre-war design development. The railways also had to contend with difficult economic conditions after the war that culminated in the Wall Street Crash of 1929, which restricted investment. By the mid-1930s, as the Art Deco style took hold, new futuristic locomotives and rolling stock began to be introduced, inspired not only by the hunger to develop the steam engine to its fullest potential, but also out of economic necessity. The rise of long-distance air travel and the beginnings of mass car ownership began to seriously affect railway business, particularly on long-distance and luxury services.

The rise of high-speed streamlined express trains was also supported by clever marketing and public relations on the part of the railway companies; they competed against one another and with European rivals to operate the 'world's fastest train'. On the GWR, it seemed that the company appeared content to run express trains like the 'Cornish Riviera Limited' in much the same way as it had done for years, providing a reliable, comfortable and relatively profitable service; however, in June 1932 the GWR was able to score a significant public relations coup when a new record for its 'Cheltenham Flyer' express was achieved. The train, hauled by No. 5006 *Tregenna Castle*, covered the stretch between Swindon and Paddington in 56 minutes 47 seconds at an average speed of 81.7 mph.

The name 'Cheltenham Flyer' was not the official title of the service; introduced in 1923, it was recorded in GWR timetables as the 'Cheltenham Spa Express'. The afternoon service from Cheltenham to Paddington via Gloucester and Stroud was a fairly leisurely affair until it reached Swindon, and the company's boast that the 'Cheltenham Flyer' was the 'world's fastest train' could only be applied to the Swindon–Paddington section of the service and was based on average rather than maximum speeds. When introduced, it snatched the 'Blue Riband' speed record from the LNER with a 75 minute journey from Swindon to London, a timing that was steadily reduced over the next nine years.

A striking Art Deco style London & North Eastern Railway poster, produced in 1935 to promote the 'Silver Jubilee' service. (SSPL)

Normal timings for the service were slightly slower than the record run of *Tregenna Castle* but, in October 1932, the GWR reduced the timing of the train from 67 to 65 minutes from Swindon. While passengers travelling to Paddington still enjoyed a rapid non-stop trip to the capital, the hold on the 'world's fastest train' record would be short-lived for the 'Cheltenham Flyer', as streamlined competition from both the LNER and German and American diesel trains steadily relegated the service. By 1939 it was not even in the top 100 fastest recorded runs.

Given the exemplary performance of its locomotives on expresses like the 'Cheltenham Flyer' and the 'Bristolian' (inaugurated in August 1935) without the need for streamlining, it

Left: The 'Cheltenham Flyer', styled as the 'World's Fastest Train' before the coming of LMS and LNER streamlined designs. **Below**: A special luggage label issued to passengers on the 'Cheltenham Flyer' service in the 1930s. (STEAM)

is perhaps slightly surprising that the first real example of streamlining being introduced on British railways was on two GWR engines. In April 1935 the company showed off a heavily modified 4-6-0 King Henry VII at Swindon; the seven-year old engine had a bulbous nose cone modified cab and streamlined fairings fitted to its footplate. A second engine, *Manorbier Castle*, was given the same treatment by Chief Mechanical Engineer C. B. Collett in May but the design seems crude – even comical – in comparison with the elegant A4 Pacifics that would emerge from Doncaster works within months.

The GWR publicity department had noted that 'streamlining is becoming more and more insisted on by all forms of transport' and there is little doubt that, by 1935, it was becoming the vogue. Car designers such as Geddes and Raymond Loewy had pioneered its use on motorcars and, by the early 1930s, railway engineers were enthusiastically embracing the idea. Although there were some notable high-speed diesel trains, such as the French Bugatti railcar introduced in 1932 and the German 'Flying Hamburger', which entered service three

A wooden pattern from Swindon Railway Works for casting a headboard of the GWR and BR (W) Express the 'Bristolian'. (Great Central Railwayana Auctions)

years later, steam technology still predominated in an age where iconic locomotives and trains were produced offering speed and style to passengers.

Streamlined trains were built and operated in mainland Europe and in the United States to great effect but, in Great Britain, it was on the London & North Eastern Railway that it was most widely used. Three famous streamlined expresses – the 'Silver Link', the 'Coronation' and the 'West Riding Limited' – were among the fastest and most luxurious in the world, their significance only diminished by the outbreak of war in 1939. While Charles Collett had toyed with streamlining at Swindon, it was Sir Nigel Gresley, the Chief Mechanical Engineer of the LNER, who was its greatest proponent on British railways. Given the success of diesel traction elsewhere, there was some debate about the suitability of streamlined steam and, as a result, before designs were produced, two high-speed trials using Gresley A3 Pacifics on lightweight trains were undertaken. These were followed by wind tunnel research to reduce wind resistance and to ensure that steam and smoke from the locomotive would not obscure the driver's view.

The whole process took place over an extraordinarily short period of time, with the first of the steam trials taking place in November 1934 and the new engine first steamed in September 1935. Gresley's A4 Pacific has been described as one of the most graceful and stylish engines ever built, but it must have seemed quite alien and unorthodox to many railwaymen used to more workaday designs.

Great Western Railway locomotive No. 5005 *Manorbier Castle*, originally built in 1927, stands outside Swindon Works after streamlining in 1935. The design seems crude in comparison to LNER and LMS designs, and was largely removed within five years.

On 27 September 1935, the new 'Silver Jubilee' express undertook a demonstration run between King's Cross and Grantham. On the journey the train created four world records, and twice attained a maximum speed of 112 ½ miles an hour.

It was intended that the A4 locomotives would haul a brand new express, 'The Silver Jubilee', named to mark the Silver Jubilee of King George V in 1935. As work on the new engines progressed at Doncaster, orders for new rolling stock were placed; initially, the train consisted of two articulated two-car carriages, along with a triple restaurant car and kitchen unit. An additional carriage was added three years later to increase capacity. The carriages were clad in steel, covered in an elegant silver-grey 'rexine' fabric with stainless steel trim, and the first four engines – *Silver Link*, *Quicksilver*, *Silver King* and *Silver Fox* – were all painted the same shade. Art Deco styling dominated the interior, with chrome-plated metal fittings and 'jazz' patterned seats, although many commentators described it as 'comfortable rather than streamlined'.

The train was an immediate success after its launch in September 1935. The southbound train left Newcastle at 10.00 a.m., arriving at King's Cross in just 4 hours. The return trip started at 5.30 p.m., with Newcastle being reached at 9.30 p.m. It was so popular that passengers without a reservation were unlikely to find a seat on the train, despite the fact that a supplement of 5 shillings first class and 3 shillings third class was payable on top of the ordinary fare. Running only on weekdays, it was estimated that, within two years, these

No. 2511 *Silver King*, the third of four LNER A4 Pacifics painted with the distinctive silver-grey-and-charcoal livery, at the head of the 'Silver Jubilee' train.

supplements had already paid for the cost of the train; with the outbreak of war, the service was withdrawn, and it was never reinstated.

The success of the 'Silver Jubilee' was not replicated by sister train 'Coronation', introduced in 1937. Connecting King's Cross and Edinburgh Waverley, this streamlined express service was bigger and more than 40 per cent heavier than the 'Jubilee'. It too

A composite postcard image, produced to advertise the new LNER 'Coronation' express; it includes a photograph of the very distinctive 'beaver tail' observation car. Dark winter weather meant that this feature was less popular and well-used than the company anticipated. (STEAM)

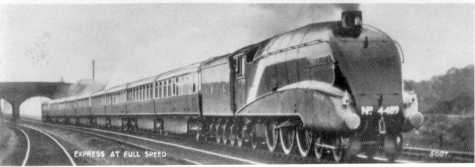

The graceful lines of Gresley A4 Pacific *Bittern*. In June 2013 the engine set a speed record for a preserved steam locomotive of 92.8 mph. (Mike Freeman)

had a striking appearance, the nine-coach train consisting of four articulated carriages completed by a unique 'beaver-tail' observation car. This was equipped with armchairs but these were only available to passengers willing to pay an additional fee of a shilling per hour; in the winter months the car was not attached, as much of the journey took place in darkness. The exterior of the carriages were painted in a two-tone blue livery, the darker 'Garter Blue' matching the livery of the A4 Pacifics that hauled the service. The inside of the train was more innovative in design than that of the 'Silver Jubilee', with a pressure ventilation system enabling carriages to have sealed windows; extra insulation was also provided to make the journey as quiet as possible.

Both services were afternoon departures, aimed at serving the needs of the businessman. The up train, leaving London at 4.00 p.m., ran non-stop to York, timetabled to do this portion of the journey at an average of 71.9 mph, before arriving in the Scottish capital at 10.00 p.m. On the southbound journey the train left Edinburgh at

WEST RIDING LTD. POTTER BAR SOUTH.

The third of the LNER's streamlined expresses was the 'West Riding Limited'. Looking very like its sister train, the 'Coronation', but without an observation car, the train passes Potters bar with Gresley A4 Pacific *Golden Shuttle* in charge. (STEAM)

4.30 p.m., arriving at King's Cross at 10.30 p.m. Despite the glamorous setting for the service and its high average speed, it failed to grab the public imagination in the way the 'Silver Jubilee' did. Punctuality and reliability were not always as good as they should be, and passenger receipts were poor. Matters were only improved with the addition of a stop at Newcastle early in 1938. Like its more successful rival, the train was not revived after the war, instead being replaced by a new train, the 'Talisman', some seventeen years after its demise.

The third LNER streamlined express was the 'West Riding Limited', introduced in October 1937. The train ran from King's Cross to Leeds, leaving the capital at 7.10 p.m. and running via Doncaster to Leeds central, arriving there at 9.53 p.m. It then reversed and ran the 9 miles to Bradford, arriving 18 minutes later. While the bulk of the journey was done with an A4 Pacific in charge, as a consequence of the steep gradients on the

Did you know?

Away from the East Coast Main Line, the LNER introduced one final streamlined express in 1937. The 'East Anglian' was a luxury service linking Liverpool Street, Ipswich and Norwich. It was reported that new rolling stock produced for the train was 'neither articulated nor streamlined' but it was hauled by B17 4-6-0 locomotives specially modified to resemble one of Gresley's A4 Pacifics.

No. 6220, the *Coronation Scot*. The Distinctive lining on the streamlined boiler casing was continued along the carriage stock. (STEAM)

Leeds–Bradford section, two rather more humble tank engines were usually used on that section of line.

The rolling stock used was identical to that used on the 'Coronation' and, for a time, in honour of the region's wool industry, two A4 locomotives with fitting names – *Golden Fleece* and *Golden Shuttle* – were allocated to the service. Like the other streamliners, the West Riding Limited did not return after the war but, in 1949, a new train titled simply the 'West Riding' began running between King's Cross, Leeds and Bradford, surviving in various forms until the early 1960s.

In an echo of the rivalry of 'Race to the North', the London, Midland & Scottish Railway produced their own streamlined express service in 1937 as a riposte to the exploits of their rivals over the Pennines. The 'Coronation Scot' linked London Euston and Glasgow Central stations, the train pausing briefly at Carlisle for a crew change and to allow passengers to

THE "CORONATION SCOT"

The driver leans out of the cab of the 'Coronation Scot' as it speeds towards Glasgow.

In 1939, 'Coronation Scot' was sent to the United States to attend the New York 'World's Fair'. This commemorative postcard shows the engine next to a New Haven streamlined 4-6-4 locomotive. (STEAM)

board and leave the train. With a journey time of 6 hours 30 minutes, the service could not match the speed of the LNER's Coronation service, but gradients made the route more challenging, especially North of Crewe.

The train featured new, streamlined 4-6-2 locomotives designed by William Stanier. Test runs for the new service had been carried out with one of the Princess Elizabeth class, but the new engines were bigger and featured a striking aerodynamic casing that had been devised at Derby Works following wind tunnel testing. On a trial run in 1937 the first of the class, No. 6220, achieved a top speed of 114 mph. The first six engines were painted in a distinctive blue livery, similar to that used on the old Caledonian Railway, while the rest featured the more traditional Crimson Lake livery used on the rest of the LMS locomotive fleet. All the locomotives carried an Art Deco lining along the streamlined casing that was repeated on the nine-coach train they hauled. Unlike the LNER, the LMS did not build new carriages for the Coronation Scot but instead used existing carriage stock for the launch of the train in 1937.

Did you know?

A number of special trains organised for publicity purposes produced some high-speed runs that, while exciting for reporters, caused some disquiet among railway staff. On 29 June 1937 a press run for the LMS 'Coronation Scot' service almost ended in disaster despite the train touching 114 mph on its journey. Braking hard as it approached Crewe, it was still racing at more than 52 mph as it ran through the station, sending crockery crashing to the floor of the dining car as it did so.

A4 Pacific *Union of South Africa* speeds past the cameraman on a main line special on 18 June 2006. (Mike Freeman)

5
Boat and Mail Trains

For many the classic image of the boat train is that of a 1930s express like the 'Golden Arrow', leaving Victoria bound for the Continent full of passengers looking as if they had stepped from the pages of an Agatha Christie novel. In fact, train services timed to connect with steamers running from Britain to Ireland and the Continent had been running since the 1840s. The earliest trains connecting with steamers were operated by the London & Blackwall Railway, which ran services to Blackwall Pier, from where ships departed for the Continent. These did not directly connect with boat departures but, within a few years, formal arrangements had developed at ports like Dover and Folkestone, where cross-Channel steamships connected with trains from the capital. The Southern Railway called the brief voyage from these South East ports the 'short sea route'

London, Brighton & South Coast Railway H1 4-4-2 No. 40 on a Pullman boat train service at Balham before the First World War. (STEAM)

Battle of Britain class 4-6-2 *Tangmere* recreates the glory days of the 'Night Ferry' on the 'Canterbury Belle' steam special on 9 May 2013. (Ashley Smith)

and passengers for the Continent began their journey at Victoria. Before the creation of the Southern, in the latter part of the nineteenth century the London, Chatham & Dover and South Eastern Railways offered a variety of boat trains via Dover and Folkestone, competing fiercely for traffic. The two companies amalgamated in 1899 and Pullman carriages were introduced in 1910.

After Grouping, the Southern rationalised Continental boat train services, confirming Victoria as the sole departure point for Paris trains. By 1930 the SR were operating fifteen boat trains between Victoria and Dover and Folkestone including the 'Golden Arrow'. After the 'Golden Arrow', the best-known Continental boat train of this era was the 'Night Ferry', a service that was unique in that it was operated using French 'Wagon-Lits' sleeper carriages built to run on the restricted loading gauge of British lines. These enabled passengers to board the train at Victoria, travel through the night, and arrive in the French capital without having to change. Brand-new ferry facilities were built at Dover and Dunkirk, allowing the twelve-coach boat trains to be shunted on and off three new ferries that had also been constructed for the service. The 'Night Ferry' began operation in October 1936 and was a well-patronised train, surviving until the 1980s, by which time cheaper air travel and competition from cross-Channel ferries had reduced passenger numbers significantly.

Another constituent of the Southern, the London & South Western Railway, ran boat trains out of Waterloo station, an operation that continued after Grouping in 1923. Trains ran to Southampton and Plymouth, but differed to those using the 'Short Sea Route' since they largely served liners calling at both ports. The docks at Southampton were also owned by the Southern and were extensively redeveloped in the 1930s, attracting more ocean liner traffic. By the 1950s over 6,500 boat trains were handled at Southampton annually; special trains were introduced by British Railways – the '*Cunarder*' named for the 'Queen Elizabeth' and 'Queen Mary' and the '*Statesman*' introduced to carry passengers from the 'United States' line.

The LSWR and the GWR had also competed briefly at the beginning of the twentieth century in a battle to secure 'Ocean Mail' traffic from Plymouth. Although most liners called at Southampton to discharge passengers and mail, the passage up the English Channel could be slow, and some liners made a brief stop at Plymouth Sound, where mail and passengers were ferried to trains waiting on the dockside. Special services were run at high speed to London and it was only a serious accident at Salisbury involving a LSWR train that ended a period of intense rivalry, which had led to some

A poster produced by British Railways in 1959 advertises the 'Night Ferry' sleeping car train to Paris and Brussels. (SSPL)

The 'American Boat Express' train, run by the London & South Western Railway and pictured in this vintage postcard, features conventional rather than Pullman carriage stock. (STEAM)

A beautiful photograph taken by the company photographer from the footbridge at Paddington station in November 1929. Passengers and admirers look at the gleaming Pullman stock, which is being used on the 'Ocean Mail' service to Plymouth. (STEAM)

very fast running of express trains by both companies. The lessons learned, particularly by the GWR, were used in future expresses like the 'Cornish Riviera Limited'.

Both the GWR and later the Southern also competed for more modest Channel Island business, running trains to connect with ferries to the 'Sunshine Isles' of Jersey and Guernsey. Boat trains from Paddington ran to Weymouth to connect with steamers and Southern expresses terminated at Southampton, where similar services were run to the Channel Isles. In 1906 the Great Western opened a brand-new harbour at Fishguard in West Wales. Costing almost £1 million it could handle large numbers of passengers bound for Southern Ireland and the company had ambitions to develop Fishguard as an ocean terminal, with liners from New York calling there ahead of Liverpool, Plymouth or Southampton. Special boat trains were run to Paddington as the port attracted ships from the Cunard and Blue Funnel line, but the business attracted was short-lived and, after the First World War, liners went back to calling at Plymouth, Southampton and Liverpool.

Did you know?

Before 1923, the London & North Western Railway ran 'American Specials' non-stop between Liverpool (Riverside) and Euston. These trains continued in LMS days but between the two wars the port of Liverpool lost ground to Southampton as first port of call for transatlantic liners. As a result, while Euston still handled some ocean passenger traffic, the focus shifted to the Southern, where, in addition to its timetabled boat trains, it also supplied special trains from Southampton and Dover where required.

Above left: The front of a delightful publicity leaflet, issued jointly by the GWR and Southern Railways to advertise their services to the Channel Island of Guernsey. (Great Western Trust Didcot)
Above right: A 1912 Great Eastern Railway poster with artwork by Norman Wilkinson advertising services to Belgium, Denmark, Germany, Holland and Sweden via its facilities at Harwich. (SSPL)

On the LNER, boat trains largely operated on ex-Great Eastern Railway lines. The 'Continentals' ran from Liverpool Street to Harwich Parkeston Quay and connected with ships operated by the LNER and also Danish and Dutch shipping lines. In 1924 the company invested in two new trains for the 'Hook Continental', building further new stock in 1938. The train left London at 8.30 p.m., followed by Antwerp, Flushing and Scandinavian Continental expresses. Further north, the Great Central and, later, the LNER operated boat trains from Hull and Immingham, even connecting with shipping lines bound for Scandinavia from the Commission Quay on the River Tyne.

The London & North Western Railway and, later, the LMS ran the 'Irish Mail', an express service linking the capital and the North Wales port of Holyhead. The first proper services carrying mail and passengers began in 1848, when the Chester–Holyhead line was completed, and the 'Irish Mail' was inaugurated on 1 August of that year. Trains left Euston at 8.45 p.m., arriving 9 long hours later at 6.45 the following morning. Despite this arduous journey, the service was the successor to horse-drawn mail coaches, which had taken up to two days before the coming of railways! Despite the best efforts of both the LNWR and LMS, it was not until 1920 that the railway was able to acquire the contract to operate ships across the Irish Sea from the City of Dublin Steam Packet Co. The service continued to operate into BR days, and can now rightly be called Britain's first 'named' train.

To reach the Irish sea port of Holyhead, London & North Western Railway (and later LMS and BR) trains needed to cross the Menai Straits using Telford's iconic Britannia Bridge, which opened in 1850. (STEAM)

An exterior view of a British Railways (Western Region) Travelling Post Office carriage. The net for the collection of mail bags en route is very apparent; also visible is the unusual offset corridor connection. (STEAM)

While boat trains like the 'Irish Mail' and specials run from ports like Southampton and Plymouth were vitally important for the rapid transit of mail delivered from destinations in Europe or farther afield, railways also played a vital role in moving domestic mail around the country, using a network of travelling post offices that by the 1950s covered about 2.5 million miles per year. The Royal Mail had been quick to see the potential of railways as a way of transporting mail, and the first Travelling Post Office (TPO) was introduced on the Grand Junction Railway in 1838. The postal network grew as fast as the railway network, and there were soon TPO carriages in use on most main lines. The next logical development was the introduction of the first train carrying mail only; this took place on the GWR Bristol–Paddington route in 1855, although it was another thirty years before a similar service between London and Scotland was established.

Trains were assembled according to the route they served, but in general included a number of coaches where mail could be sorted, as well as vans for the storage of already-sorted mail and parcels. The sorting coaches were normally arranged to give maximum movement and comfort for postal staff in a very confined space. Fittings were padded to save sorters from knocks and bumps as the trains swayed at speed. Each had their own job to do, but they worked as a team; they were experienced people with encyclopaedic knowledge of British cities, towns, villages and even the suburbs and scattered hamlets within them. In an average run, a team of around thirty-four postal staff could handle more than 2,000 bags of mail and 90,000 separate items as the train raced through the night.

Mail was picked up en route using what became known as an exchange apparatus; the mechanism, using an arm and nets to collect and deposit mail bags at speed, was developed in the 1830s and, by the early twentieth century, there were almost 250 locations where exchange could take place. Where larger amounts of mail needed to be collected or delivered, trains stopped with other services timetabled to meet as they did at Bristol on the Western route, when the TPO was involved in an exchange of mail with eight other TPOs just after midnight.

The interior of Great Western Railway letter sorting van No. 806, photographed by the company in July 1932. (STEAM)

Left: A member of railway staff waits by the track as a Great Eastern Railway mail train approaches the pick-up point. (STEAM)
Below: The cameraman is close to the action, with a London & North Western Railway mail train being about to pick up a load of mail bags at full speed. (STEAM)

PICKING UP MAIL BAGS AT FULL SPEED

Did you know?

The Travelling Post Office service operated by the London Midland & Scottish railway from Euston to Glasgow inspired one of the most famous British documentary films of the twentieth century: *Night Mail*. Produced for the Post Office in 1936, the evocative and atmospheric film was directed by Harry Watt and Basil Wright, and was provided with a poetic coda by W. H. Auden that has become famous in its own right and also features music by Benjamin Britten.

Mail trains generally ran at night and, as a result, most of the public were unaware of their importance. And, while mail trains carried only postal staff and not passengers, they were in the truest sense 'express trains' and always given top priority by signalling staff since, if they were delayed, a large amount of people would be affected if letters and parcels did not arrive in good time. The growth of road transport gradually eroded the importance of express mail services on railways and, by the 1960s, the Royal Mail was increasingly using lorries to move mail and parcels. The Anglo-Scottish TPOs were abandoned in 1993 and, despite investment in a new containerised Railnet system soon after that, which involved the maintenance of the surviving twenty-four TPO services and new trains, Royal Mail announced it would stop using rail for mail in 2003. The last TPO ran in January 2004, although a limited amount of mail is still carried by rail today.

A Royal Mail lorry is visible behind this huge pile of mail bags at Paddington, pictured in 1926. (STEAM)

6
Other Express Services

While so much attention is paid to famous named trains, it must not be forgotten that British railways ran large numbers of other important regional and cross-country express services. Not all were named, but they nevertheless provided links between important towns and cities away from the capital. There is simply not space here to detail all the main line express services provided by the pre-Grouping and Big Four companies and, subsequently, the nationalised British railways named or un-named, but they provided the bulk of passenger income generated for the railways on a day-to-day basis. Excursion and special traffic also provided an opportunity for railways to run additional express services to transport holidaymakers in the summer months and others to attend sporting and other events all year round.

The 'Torbay Express' was introduced in 1923 and ran between Paddington and Kingswear until 1968. (Great Central Railwayana Auctions)

The busy scene at King's Cross, while showing No. 2570 *Call Boy* departing with the 'Flying Scotsman', also features two more Gresley Pacifics waiting to depart with regional express services. (STEAM)

The North British Hotel at Edinburgh Waverley dominates the background of this postcard view, depicting a NBR East Coast main line express leaving the Scottish capital around 1914. (STEAM)

Although many of the regional services were fast trains, they naturally made more station stops than the more famous expresses. Linking up the main lines radiating from London, trains were often jointly operated by a number of railway companies because of the route and distance travelled. An early example of a fast train of this type was the 'Ports to Ports Express'. The title was unofficial and used by railway staff and travellers, but not named in timetables.

The LMS Black Five class designed by William Stanier soon gained a reputation as a 'maid of all work' after its introduction in 1934. It was used extensively on express passenger and cross-country services. No. 45305 is based on the Great Central Railway, where it was photographed on 5 June 2015. (Mike Freeman)

Inaugurated in 1906, the express was one of a series of trains that had been introduced that linked the North East of England with the South West and Wales since the 1890s.

Initially the train was to run between the industrial ports of Newcastle and Barry. Not surprisingly, many of the passengers were ships' crew travelling from one ship to another and the train was soon extended to continue westwards to Swansea, another large docks complex. The train, which included a restaurant car, consisted of GWR and LNER rolling stock, used on alternate days. It left Newcastle at 9.30 a.m. and called at York, Sheffield, Nottingham, Leicester, Banbury, Cheltenham, Gloucester, Newport and Cardiff, arriving at Swansea at 11.45 p.m. – a journey of well over 11 hours. This was despite the long journey being made shorter by the train opting for a rather unusual shortcut across country between Banbury and Cheltenham, taking the single-track line that linked the sleepy Cotswolds towns of Chipping Norton, Stow-on-the-Wold and Bourton-on-the-Water.

Another train using the route between the North East and Banbury was the Newcastle–Bournemouth express, which needed three Big Four companies to operate it. Leaving Newcastle at 7.30 a.m., the train, composed of Southern Railway stock, ran via Sunderland, Darlington and York and then on to Banbury, arriving there at 2.17 p.m. A GWR locomotive then took the train to Basingstoke via Oxford and Didcot, where a Southern engine was then coupled on for the final leg of the journey to Bournemouth. The south coast resort was finally reached at 6.27 p.m. The LNER also ran another long-distance service from Newcastle that enabled passengers from the North to connect with Channel Island steamships at Southampton. This used GWR and LNER carriages on alternate days, but passengers may not have enjoyed the experience quite so much after Leicester, where loaded fish wagons that had just arrived from Grimsby were added to the train. To make matters worse, there was no restaurant car after Oxford, which must have made the last part of the 10-hour trip seem never-ending.

An ex-LNWR Claughton 4-6-0 hauls an un-named express in the 1920s before the introduction of larger and more powerful Fowler engines like the Royal Scot in 1927. (STEAM)

LONDON. MIDLAND SCOTTISH EXPRESS

British Railway 9F 2-10-0, although built as a heavy goods locomotive, was one of a number of the class that found fame running on the 'Pines Express'; it hauled the service on the old Somerset & Dorset route on 8 September 1962. (Mike Freeman)

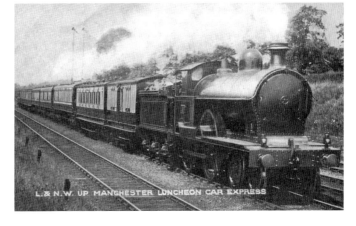

A 1910 view of a London & North Western express that ran between Euston and Manchester, providing passengers with the opportunity to take lunch on their journey. (STEAM)

The LMS also ran express services from Newcastle to the south coast via Sheffield, Derby, Birmingham and Cheltenham, using the old Somerset & Dorset Railway line to reach Poole and Bournemouth. Bournemouth was also the destination of a more famous long-distance cross-country named train: the 'Pines Express'. The train began in 1910 as a joint service operated by the London & North Western and Midland railways, linking Liverpool, Manchester and the south coast, using the Somerset & Dorset Railway from Bath onwards. At the north end of the route, the express was certainly fast, with a journey time of only 1 ¾ hours from Manchester to Birmingham.

Suspended during the First World War, the train was reinstated in peacetime and was finally given its official name by the LMS in 1927. By 1939 the journey time was just under 6 ½ hours, the southbound train running from Manchester via Crewe, Birmingham, Cheltenham and Gloucester, from where it went on to Bath. Most of the 64-mile route from Bath to Broadstone in Dorset was single track, with ferocious gradients of 1 in 50 making it a real challenge for locomotive crews.

One of the main features of these north-south expresses was that they avoided the complication and difficulty of travelling via London, and the necessity of changing trains and travelling between stations in the capital to join connecting services. The 'Sunny South

The English Electric prototype Type 5 Co-Co diesel-electric *Deltic* prepares to leave London King's Cross for Leeds in 1959 on the 'White Rose' service. (53A Models of Hull Collection)

The postcard's photographer has captured this 1950s scene at Paddington, just prior to the departure of the 'Cambrian Coast Express' at 10.20 p.m. The train called at Leamington Spa, Birmingham Snow Hill, Wolverhampton, Welshpool, Machynlleth and Dovey Junction, arriving in Aberystwyth just before 4 p.m.

Express' was a direct result of requests from travellers in the Midlands and North of England for direct trains to holiday resorts on the South Coast; the first service, begun modestly in 1904 with the provision of through carriages between Manchester and Brighton, soon developed the following year into a proper express service, which was run by the London & North Western and London, Brighton & South Coast railways.

Although beginning as a daily service, after the First World War the express was a weekend-only train except during the height of the holiday season. The 'Sunny South' route avoided the centre of the capital by using the West London line that ran through Kensington Addison Road, Clapham Junction and East Croydon, with Brighton being reached in under 8 hours. In the summer months, additional services were also run on the route to Eastbourne, Hastings and Kent coastal resorts such as Herne Bay, Ramsgate and Margate.

For the railways it was at bank holidays and during the summer holiday period that express train working was at its most difficult and complicated. The sheer number of passengers wishing to travel every Easter, Whitsun and August bank holiday as well as on peak summer Saturdays meant that often the published timetables were suspended or varied. Many of the

Right: A 1926 handbill issued by the GWR, advertising an 'express' excursion to London.

most famous named expresses like the 'Cornish Riviera Limited' could be run in duplicate or even triplicate, and other special services were run. In addition, these busy holiday periods could be complicated by large events such as sporting occasions like the FA Cup final, all of which required additional trains to carry passengers who needed to be taken to their destination and returned home the same day.

Fast excursion trains for such events could be a great source of income for railways, particularly in the era before car ownership began to erode their business. The Grand National held at Aintree required more than sixty trains to bring punters to the event in the 1930s, with most arriving in an intense 90-minute period between 11.30 a.m. and 1.30 p.m. Trains originated from all over the country, including three London termini, Glasgow, Carlisle, Nottingham, Gloucester and Bristol. The St Leger race meeting held near Doncaster provided similar logistical challenges for the LNER, with more than fifty special excursion trains arriving there on the morning of the event, traffic being heavier from the North than the South.

An unidentified ex-GWR Castle class engine is at the head of a special excursion train run from Paddington to visit the Land Rover production facility at Solihull. The picture is undated, but was probably taken in the late 1950s. (British Motor Industry Heritage Trust)

Even more challenging were the arrangements required to cope with football matches and other events. Following the opening of Wembley Stadium in 1923 the organisational skills of railway management were tested to the full, and the FA Cup final that year played between Bolton Wanderers and West Ham saw more than 270,000 people transported on special trains. The LMS ran sixty-nine specials, the LNER forty-three, the GWR twenty-four and the Southern just six. Getting football supporters to the game was difficult enough, but the railways then had to get them home in good time, and so it was not surprising that the *Railway Magazine* described the day as 'one of the greatest transport feats ever achieved'. While passenger numbers were never quite as high as they were for events like the cup final, railway companies still ran high-speed excursion trains for large-scale public events such as royal coronations, funerals and jubilee celebrations, seaside and Christmas illuminations, and agricultural shows, fetes and military tattoos.

Did you know?

Although few goods trains ever carried a headboard, with the exception of a small number provided with these for publicity purposes, it is probably not well known that many express freight services were named. The names were usually only known to staff or enthusiasts and usually reflected either the kind of freight carried, or the route served. Thus the Kidderminster–Paddington service was the 'Carpet' in honour of that town's principal trade and the 'Grocer' was a general train carrying tea, coffee, cocoa and margarine that ran from London to Aberdeen.

A very early aeroplane has been superimposed into this pre-First World War postcard of a London & South Western Railway express. (STEAM)

7
Express Train Innovation

As the premier service on any railway, the express train (and especially the named express) tended to feature the most modern locomotives and rolling stock, supported by other innovations and features both on and off the train. These expresses were seen by railway management as not only sources of revenue, but also as great public relations opportunities to showcase the progress of the business. This became ever more important in the 1920s and 1930s, when the Big Four companies competed strongly with each other.

It was, of course, hardly surprising that railways would use the completion of a new and powerful express passenger engine to support and advertise its services. In 1924 both the LNER and GWR exhibited locomotives at the British Empire Exhibition at Wembley with 'Flying Scotsman' and 'Caerphilly Castle' displayed close together in the Palace of Engineering. Both had been completed recently and were seen as the vanguard for both companies. The emphasis in the 1920s was on locomotive *power* and in August 1926 the Southern

Above left: Looking at the massive proportions of the engine reproduced here, it was no wonder that the Southern Railway boasted that their new Lord Nelson class locomotive was the 'most powerful in the world' when introduced in 1925.

Above right: The cover of the Great Western Railway's book about its express locomotive, the *Caerphilly Castle*. The book was published in 1924 and reprinted a number of times.

Railway had announced that their new Lord Nelson class 4-6-0 was the most powerful engine on British railways, developing a nominal tractive effort of 33,500 lbs. This spurred Great Western Railway management to ask C. B. Collett, their Chief Mechanical Engineer at Swindon, to do better and so, in the following year, the first King class locomotive, *King George V*, was built at Swindon with a tractive effort of 40,300 lbs. Part of the publicity campaign to launch the engine was its first appearance on the 'Cornish Riviera Limited' in July 1927.

The Royal Scot class of locomotive, also introduced by the LMS in 1927, provided the motive power for the company's premier express until 1933 when they were replaced by more powerful Princess Royal and later Coronation locomotives. With the development of streamlining, the emphasis changed from power to speed, and the GWR and Southern railways were unable to compete with the exploits of the LNER and LMS as they battled to hold the world speed record for steam locomotives. Ultimately Gresley's East Coast racers, his A4 Pacifics, were pre-eminent, despite the LMS initially breaking the record in June 1937 with a speed of 114 mph on a press run for the 'Coronation Scot'. Just over a year later, on July 1938, No. 4468 *Mallard* set an unbroken record for steam traction of 126 mph, effectively ending the rivalry between the two companies, and providing a massive public relations boost for the LNER.

The successful running of high-speed express services also relied on some rather less sophisticated but no less important equipment, such as water troughs. In the 1860s, as non-stop trains became more numerous and speeds increased, the major factor restricting the progress of expresses was how locomotives could be supplied with water without them stopping. The problem was solved by John Ramsbottom of the L&NWR, who devised a system using troughs laid between the tracks from which water could be drawn at speed through using a scoop attached to the tender that was lowered by the engine crew. Most railways in England, with the exception of the LSWR, adopted the system and, by the 1920s, there were troughs along most main lines. For non-stop expresses like the 'Flying Scotsman' and 'Coronation Scot', these were vital; despite the fact that locomotives had large tenders carrying thousands of gallons of water, high-speed running was thirsty work.

The solid lines of Royal Scot Class 4-6-0 *Grenadier Guardsman* are apparent in this coloured illustration, taken from a children's railway book of the 1920s.

L.&.N.W. IRISH MAIL TAKING WATER AT BUSHEY TROUGHS.

Above: The water cascading from the back of the tender of the London & North Western 4-4-0 indicates that the fireman has dropped the scoop to collect water at Bushey Troughs on the main line from Euston to Birmingham. (STEAM)
Below right: A GWR Saint class locomotive, No. 2934 *Butleigh Court* takes water at troughs, watched by the fireman of a goods train as it passes on the main line.

For the LMS, the fact that water trough development had begun on one of its constituent companies meant that its West Coast route was well provided with no fewer than eleven sets of troughs between Euston and Glasgow. On the East Coast Main Line, provision was less generous and there were only six sets of troughs between London and Edinburgh, with the section between Doncaster and the Scottish capital, a distance of nearly 250 miles, only having two in all. Lower water consumption by superheated GWR locomotives meant that there were only fourteen sets of troughs on the whole system, with four on the route of the 'Cornish Riviera Limited', five on the South Wales Main Line and three on the Birmingham route.

The process of 'taking water' required considerable skill on the part of the locomotive fireman, who needed to ensure

that, when reaching the troughs, he dropped the scoop at the correct point and that he raised it once the right amount of water had been collected. Too little water might entail an enforced stop further down the line, which would incur the wrath of railway management, but letting the tender overfill would lead to water overflowing and cascading over the first carriage. Any passengers who had neglected to close their windows might then receive an unwelcome drenching.

Did you know?

In 1937 an LNER inspector riding on the footplate of the 'Coronation' express was killed when northbound and southbound trains passed each other at Wiske Moor water troughs near York. Water overflowing from the trains with a combined speed of 140 mph caused a surge that shattered the cab window. Engines were subsequently modified and provided with armour-plated cab glass.

Another innovation aiding high-speed running was the slip coach. This enabled carriages on trains to be detached while the train was travelling at full speed, providing passengers wishing to alight at intermediate stations with the chance to do so. The London, Brighton & South Coast Railway began experimenting with the idea early in 1858, closely followed by the GWR, and by 1914 many of the major railways had introduced slip coaches on their express services. By 1936 the GWR was the only company to still use slip carriages; that year the remaining services operated by the LNER on their Great Central and Great Eastern sections were replaced with stopping trains.

Slip coaches were equipped with a guard's compartment at one end, and it was from there that he could release a 'slip-hook' coupling, allowing the carriage to be detached from the main train; the carriage was provided with its own independent braking system, enabling it to coast safely to a halt in the station. The carriages, although providing passengers with the chance to travel on high-speed trains, were not universally popular as the guard's

A GWR slip coach in action. The main train is racing on towards its destination while the guard applies the brakes on the carriage. Each slip coach had its own independent braking system; a set of brake cylinders can be seen underneath the carriage in this photograph. (STEAM)

compartment meant that there was no access to the restaurant car for those travelling in slip portions, a disadvantage on longer-distance trains.

On long journeys, passenger facilities on trains were important, with railways competing not only in terms of speed but also in comfort and luxury; not surprisingly, most of the major developments in carriage design were introduced on express trains. Gangway connections between carriages were introduced on the GWR in 1882 and the first corridor service on the same railway a decade later. Steam heating and the widespread use of lavatories on main line trains also dated from the 1890s. Carriage stock used on premier expresses was, therefore, of the highest quality and in later years included double-glazed windows, electric lighting, new heating and ventilation systems, and well-designed, elegant interiors. By the 1930s, most of new carriages built or used on LNER and LMS expresses like the 'Flying Scotsman', 'Royal Scot' or 'Coronation Scot' also incorporated end-only doors, replacing the compartment doors common to older corridor train stock, and there was also a move to build carriages with 'open' saloon interiors or smaller four-seat compartments, which helped make them seem lighter and more airy.

The elegant lines of Gresley LNER teak restaurant car No 7960 are seen at King's Cross on 5 April 2016, coupled to EX-GNR N2 0-6-2 tank locomotive No. 1744. (John Pink)

The interior of a GWR restaurant car, photographed in the early 1920s. The dark interior contrasts heavily with the more modern 'Art Deco' designs that followed in the next decade.

Did you know?

For those travelling on express train services, especially on named trains, the standard of fare served could be luxurious. On the 'Silver Jubilee', passengers had the choice of no fewer than forty-six cocktails to sip while awaiting their meal; there was even one named after the train itself, which cost two shillings. The *à la carte* menu included 'real' turtle soup, Dover sole and oysters, followed by a 'Silver Jubilee Mixed Grill' with peach melba to finish.

Restaurant cars were introduced to Britain's railways in 1879, when a modified Pullman car was provided by the Great Northern Railway for its London–Leeds express service. By 1896 they, the GWR and the London & North Western, were still the only companies to provide this service. Eventually most railways provided restaurant cars on long-distance services and, excluding Pullman stock, there were well over 300 restaurant cars in use on British railways in the 1930s.

Initially facilities were provided only for first class passengers, but this practice was eventually abandoned and even the fastest and most luxurious service was open to the third class traveller. Providing high quality food in small, cramped and swaying kitchens was a real challenge to the catering staff, but they amazingly managed to produce course after course of high quality food for the hungry traveller.

Although sleeping accommodation had been provided on night trains from the 1870s onwards, the familiar layout of the sleeping carriage with a side corridor and double compartment sleeping berths was developed by the GWR in the 1890s and subsequently used by all the railways in Britain. Sleeper trains provided passengers with comfortable accommodation on long overnight journeys, especially those linking London and Scotland. There were night versions of both the 'Flying Scotsman' and the 'Royal Scot' that dated back to the nineteenth century. By the 1920s, the

A heavily stylised poster, advertising the cocktail bar on the 'Flying Scotsman', one of the numerous facilities provided for passengers on one of the most luxurious trains running on the LNER. (SSPL)

Above: Great Western branding is prominent in this view of one of its sleeping car compartments. Apart from the crested china on the left-hand side of the photograph, the bed has a blanket that features the company crest.

Right: Fittingly, it is 4-6-2 No. 4472 *Flying Scotsman* that is pictured departing from King's Cross on the 'Night Scotsman' sleeper service.

LMS express, the 'Night Scot', was a heavy train that included six or more first class sleeping cars, two third class sleepers, two dining vehicles and other carriage stock. It departed from Euston at 11.45 p.m., arriving in Glasgow at 9.35 a.m. the following day. During the Second World War the train lost its name but was still a busy service, being run in a number of portions each night. In the 1960s the train was renamed the 'Night Limited'. The LNER 'Night Scotsman' left King's Cross at 10.25 p.m., arriving at Edinburgh Waverley at 7.15 a.m., having made stops at Grantham, York and Newcastle to pick up passengers. Arriving in the Scottish capital the train was then split into three separate 'breakfast trains', serving Aberdeen, Glasgow and Perth.

Today, both East and West Coast sleeper trains have been replaced by one Anglo-Scottish sleeper service, the 'Caledonian Sleeper'. Two separate trains run each night, with a Highland service running from Euston to Edinburgh, where it splits into three further trains serving Aberdeen, Fort William and Inverness. The Lowland train travels north to Carstairs, where it splits into two, with one portion bound for Edinburgh and the other Glasgow. For travellers wishing to travel west, the 'Night Riviera' still runs seven days a week, linking London and Penzance; departing from Paddington at 11.45 p.m., the train arrives in the Cornish resort at 7.53 the following morning.

An elegant Art Deco poster, issued in 1932 by the LNER and featuring a design by the artist Robert Bartlett that promoted the 'Night Scotsman' sleeper service, which departed from King's Cross at 10.25 p.m. (SSPL)

8
What Now?

Carrying a 'Golden Arrow' headboard, SR Merchant Navy class locomotive *Clan Line* waits at the head of a steam special at London Victoria on 10 May 2015. (Mike Freeman)

While the age of the steam-hauled express train has now gone, there is still the opportunity to learn about, experience and get involved with working steam trains in museums, on heritage railways and on the main line.

Further Reading

Allen, Cecil J., *Titled Trains of Great Britain* (London: Ian Allan Ltd, 1983). *The definitive book about named expresses and their history.*

Grant, Stephen and Jeffs, Simon, *The Brighton Belle: The Story of a Famous and Much-Loved Train* (London: Capital Transport, 2012).

Harris, Michael, *British Main Line Services in the Age of Steam* (Sparkford: Oxford Publishing Company, 1996). *An overview of express passenger services run by the Big Four and British Railways.*

EXPRESS CHRISTMAS GREETINGS

LONDON & NORTH EASTERN
The 'Flying Scotsman' on the G.N. section

No doubt some lucky child was excited to receive this unusual seasonal card, which, instead of featuring a snowy Christmas scene, shows Gresley A1 Pacific No. 4475 *Flying Fox* hauling the 'Flying Scotsman'. (STEAM)

Holland, Julian, *An A–Z of Famous Express Trains* (Newton Abbot: David & Charles, 2013). *With entries for more than 120 named trains, this book is illustrated with evocative photographs and memorabilia.*

Martin, Andrew, *Belles & Whistles* (London: Profile Books, 2014). *Part-history, part-travelogue, Martin tells the story of four famous expresses: the 'Atlantic Coast Express', 'Brighton Belle', 'Cornish Riviera Express' and 'Flying Scotsman'.*

Mullay, A. J., *Streamlined Steam: Britain's 1930s Luxury Expresses* (Newton Abbot: David & Charles, 1994). *Beautifully illustrated history of the streamlined revolution on the LMS and LNER and the race to build the ultimate steam locomotive in the 1930s.*

Roden, Andrew, *The Duchesses: The Story of Britain's Ultimate Steam Locomotives* (London: Aurum Press, 2015).

Roden, Andrew, *Flying Scotsman: The Extraordinary Story of the World's Most Famous Locomotive* (London: Aurum Press, 2015). *Detailed histories of two of the most famous express locomotives used on expresses in the 1930s.*

Thomas, David St John and Whitehouse, Patrick, *The Great Days of the Express Trains* (Newton Abbot: David & Charles, 1990). *A nostalgic look back at express train travel, told through photographs and reminiscence.*

Web Resources

There are literally hundreds of websites on railway topics and, while there is no site specifically dedicated to express train services, many have information about them. Many sites for individual heritage railways include historic material as well as current information about services.

www.nrm.org.uk
The website of the National Railway Museum at York is not only packed with information about the 1 million objects the museum has in its collection, but also offers up useful links and blogs.

railways.national-forum.com
Probably the largest web forum dedicated to railway heritage, with threads and posts covering many aspects of railway history, including steam, diesel and heritage railways.

heritage-railways.com
An independent guide, giving details of more than 170 British heritage railways. It also has a useful locomotive database.

davidheyscollection.com
A nostalgic look at the golden age of steam, collecting together photographs, railwayana and memories.

flyingscotsman.org.uk
A site dedicated to the 'most famous locomotive in the world'.

The Express Train Experience
Few of the famous named trains now exist, and they are very different to those running in the steam era. The reader can instead learn more by visiting museums or heritage railways and travelling on steam rail tours on the main line.

LMS 4-6-2 *Duchess of Hamilton* stands in the Great Hall of the National Railway Museum York during a special exhibition on streamlining held there in 2009.

The crew of 4-6-2 *Oliver Cromwell* lean out from the cab of the Britannia class British Railways locomotive in a picture taken on 16 June 2013. (Mike Freeman)

Museums
There are a number of excellent museums whose collections tell the story of British express trains and display locomotives, rolling stock and memorabilia. Please check opening times before visiting!

National Railway Museum, Leeman Road, York YO24 4XJ. Tel: 08448 153139. www.nrm. org.uk

National Railway Museum Shildon, 'Locomotion', Country Durham DL4 2RE. Tel: 01904 685780. www.nrm.org.uk

Severn Valley Engine House, Highley Station, Shropshire WV16 6NZ. Tel: 01746 862387. www.svr.co.uk/EngineHouse.aspx

STEAM: Museum of the Great Western Railway, Firefly Avenue, Swindon, SN2 2EY. Tel: 01793 466646. www.steam-museum.org.uk

Heritage Railways
Listed below are some of the larger British heritage railways that are able to run the kind of locomotives and rolling stock used on express train services in the golden age of steam. A full list of railways can be found on the website of the Heritage Railways Association (www.heritagerailways.com) or the heritage railway guide (www.heritage-railways.com).

Most heritage railways also offer footplate experience courses, which allow the beginner to learn how steam locomotives work and offer the chance to fire and drive a steam engine.

The Bluebell Railway, Sheffield Park Station, East Sussex TN22 3QL. Tel: 01825 720800. www.bluebell-railway.com

One of the oldest heritage railways, the Bluebell also features the *Golden Arrow* Pullman dining train.

Didcot Railway Centre, Didcot, Oxfordshire OX11 7XJ. Tel: 01235 817200. www.didcotrailwaycentre.org.uk

A celebration of all things Great Western, based around the locomotive shed complex at Didcot. As well as live steam, there is an excellent museum that displays posters, headboards and nameplates.

The wooden head board of the '*Caledonian*', a British Railways Midland Region express introduced in 1957. (Great Central Railwayana Auctions)

Gloucester & Warwickshire Railway, The Station, Toddington, Gloucestershire GL54 5DT. Tel: 01242 621405. www.gwsr.com

The 'Honeybourne line' runs on the route of the old GWR Birmingham–Cheltenham route.

Great Central Railway, Loughborough Station, Leicestershire, LE11 1RW. Tel: 01509 632323. www.gcrailway.co.uk

The Great Central is the only double-track main line heritage railway and is one of the only places the public can experience something of what a main line was like in the age of steam.

The Mid-Hants Railway, The Railway Station, Alresford, Hampshire SO24 9JG. Tel: 01962 733810. www.watercressline.co.uk

Hampshire's Watercress Line evokes the golden age of the Southern Railway.

North Yorkshire Moors Railway, Pickering Station, North Yorkshire YO18 7AJ. www.nymr.co.uk

Large main line locomotives and Pullman dining car experience recreate the great days of express trains.

Severn Valley Railway, Kidderminster Station, Worcestershire DY10 1QR. Tel: 01562 757900. svr.co.uk

One of the largest and most successful heritage railways in the UK. The Engine House at Highley that houses the reserve collection is also worth a visit.

West Somerset Railway, The Railway Station, Minehead, Somerset TA24 5BG Tel: 01643 704996. www.westsomersetrailway.vticket.co.uk

Britain's longest heritage railway recreates the atmosphere of the GWR 'Holiday Line'.

Steam Railtours

Steam locomotives still operate chartered trains on the British main line railway network. Trips on these trains can be booked through a number of independent companies that offer different packages for the traveller. Details of steam tours can be found at uksteam.info or in railway magazines such as *Steam Railway* or the *Railway Magazine*. For the ultimate experience, the Belmond British Pullman luxury train features vintage Pullman rolling stock on a variety of fine dining experiences, day excursions and special occasion journeys, some

The lavish interior of one of the restored Pullman cars used by the Belmond Pullman Co. on steam specials. (Venice-Simplon-Orient Express Ltd)

of which are hauled by main line steam locomotives, departing London Victoria: http://www.belmond.com/british-pullman-train/luxury-train-travel.

Collecting Railwayana

While few people can afford to own their own steam locomotive, it is still possible to collect items of railway interest. Railway posters, headboards, publicity material and postcards can be obtained through internet auction sites, dealers and railway auction houses such as Great Central Railway Auctions (www.gcauctions.com).

A postcard view of an unidentified SR 'Merchant Navy' class locomotive at the head of the 'Devon Belle' express at Waterloo. The train was introduced in 1947 and, like the LNER's 'Coronation' train, also featured an observation car.

A Pullman Company poster, produced around 1935 for the LNER 'Queen of Scots' service. The artwork, produced by Septimus Scott, features an elegant female passenger wearing a suitably Scottish tartan dress. (SSPL)